William Henry Robinson

Sheffield Schoolmaster & Educationist

J.P. Craddock

Published by Cade Books

©2018 John Peter Craddock

All rights reserved.

ISBN: 978-0-9931987-5-5

John Peter Craddock has asserted his right under the Copyright, Designs and Patents Act 1988 to be identified as the author of this work.

This book is sold subject to the condition that it shall not, by way of trade or otherwise, be lent, resold, hired out, or otherwise circulated without the publisher's prior consent in any form of binding or cover other than that in which it is published and without a similar condition, including this condition, being imposed on the subsequent purchaser.

www.cadebooks.co.uk

Dedicated

to

Peter Ernest Craddock

upon

reaching

his

ninetieth year

Contents

Acknowledgements vi
Foreword vii
Introduction ix

1 Family & Early Life 1
2 Author & Father 5
3 Sheffield Federated Education Association & the Ilond ... 9
4 Presentations & Sheffield Education Week 13
5 A Rail Crash & Pipworth Road 19
6 Sharrow Lane Head & two Jubilees 23
7 Redcote & the British Association 27
8 Evacuation & the Blitz 31
9 A Long & Active Retirement 35

Family Tree 40
Photographs 41
Bibliography 53

Acknowledgements

The following have been most helpful by sharing my interest in Willie Robinson's story, providing information, references and photographs and by commenting on my work:-

Hazel Brand, Peter Craddock, Philip Craddock, Christine Hassell, Anne Hodgson, Lesley Matterson, Susan Mayock, David Robinson, Barry Swift, Elizabeth Wade & Philip Wadner

I would also like to thank the staff of the following repositories:-

Adsetts Library, Sheffield Hallam University; The British Library;

Local Studies Library, Sheffield Central Library; The National Archives;

Sheffield Archives; The Society of Genealogists & Stevenage Central Library

Foreword

I was never really aware of the impact that my grandfather had on education and the school system in general not only in Yorkshire but further afield in England. I was aware of the fact that he was a very prominent educator throughout his career and some of his achievements were proudly explained to me by my father when I was still quite young. They obviously did not register the same significance as they do now when I read about them in this book.

His range of involvements in education and some of his ideas were quite radical at the time and obviously he had to engage in a great deal of talking and persuading various hierarchies and sceptics that they would work. Not an easy task in those days but with his words of wisdom and the firmness of his personal approach and style that he was known for, he normally won the day to the enduring benefit of the entire education system at the time.

His commitment to ensuring the care and education of young children and his passionate introduction of new curricula in schools demonstrated his vision and foresight that others around him might not always have understood. It made sure that he stood out among his peers as a knowledgeable, respected innovator and reformer for a range of different and more proactive forms of education to suit the growing changes in English society at the time.

It was always a great source of excitement in my pre teenage years driving up to Sheffield from Folkestone with my sister and parents to visit Grandpa and Aunty Peggy Robinson, as Gran had died in 1948. It was sometimes even more exciting when I travelled to Sheffield by myself on the train to be met by Aunty Peggy and driven to Redcote in the grand old Lanchester saloon car which they owned at the time. I knew that Grandpa would have my special box of toys which he kept exclusively for me and that he would have a few new special jokes to tell me. Happy days at Redcote.

I am sure that Grandpa would be horrified to see the way in which certain parts of the education system have changed. Many of the values that he worked so hard to uphold and that he held so dearly in terms of early childhood education, sound Christian principles, innovation and preparation for long-term careers seem to be gradually eroding. He was a man with vision and strong beliefs; characteristics that are not easy to identify in people in this day and age.

With fondest of memories Grandpa.

David Robinson

November 2018

Introduction

Willie Robinson was my great uncle we occasionally visited at his home in Sheffield where he lived with his daughter Peggy. Once, when leaving their house, my father said to Peggy – 'John wants to know how old uncle is'. I think the answer was then a suitably impressive eighty-six.

Willie and Peggy stayed the night at our home in Malvern when they broke their journey on the way to and returning from their annual holiday. Willie made the latter particularly memorable when, just before leaving, he would kick a football around with my brother and me and palm a half-crown into each of our hands. Willie was of average height, slight build with a quiet voice that tended to whistle through his teeth, so I was surprised when my father told me that he had been a headmaster.

At Willie's eightieth birthday party in 1964, when I was six, I remember the impressive sight of a cake-board on which eighty candles burned. So many candles in close proximity caused a little concern to those aware of the potential danger. After nearly thirty-two years of retirement, Willie reached his ninety-third birthday. Both attainments were, for many years, family records.

As my interest in my family histories grew, I collected information about Willie and, from 1983, I corresponded with his son, Howard, in Australia. Then, from the 1990s, visits to the Newspaper Library in Colindale whilst pursuing other subjects, I would regularly find references to Willie in the Sheffield papers.

Slow and laborious searches of original newspapers have been revolutionized by the advent of the British Newspaper Archive (BNA) of provincial newspapers. Using the BNA, I have found several hundred references to Willie's activities with the Sheffield teaching unions, schools and other organisations during the first half of the twentieth century. Of course, the archives do not provide the full story and it should be borne in mind that Willie was not a political unionist. His affiliation to such organisations was purely to facilitate educational reform.

Brought together with personal recollections and other archival information and placed in the context of the times, I hope that the following reveals the story of a most innovative and forward thinking Sheffield schoolmaster and educationist.

John Craddock, 9 Plash Drive, Stevenage, SG1 1LW

johncraddock17@yahoo.co.uk

August 2018

Chapter One

Family & Early Life

Willie's paternal family line has been traced back to his great-great-grandfather, Thomas Robinson, who was born in the north of the Lincolnshire Fens in about 1728 and who grew up earning a modest living from the land.

In 1757 Thomas married Mary Hanson, both of Lusby, and in 1768 their son Edward was christened in the same parish. Later Edward moved south half a dozen miles to Revesby where, in 1799, he married Ann Hardy. When, in 1801, their son Thomas was christened, Edward was described as 'a small farmer and labourer' which was perhaps a small step up from father's station in life. During the period 1804 to 1816 Edward was recorded in the register as a witness to numerous marriages in Revesby. This was because, as recalled at his burial only two years after the latter date, aged only fifty, Edward was described as for 'Many years Clerk of this Parish'. Edward and Ann's oldest child, Thomas, married Hannah Mosley in 1830 and their family of nine children was brought up on a farm in Miningsby, half-way between Revesby and Lusby.

Just seven years before his father's early death, another son, Christopher, was born to Edward and Ann at Revesby in 1811. According to the 1841 census, Christopher was then a servant to a farmer and his family in Leverton, half a dozen miles to the north-east of Boston. The following year Christopher, then described as a 'cottager', married Maria Blackburn of New Bolingbroke, a dozen miles to the north of Boston. Perhaps Christopher's occupation meant that he was able to live on common land free of rent. The couple was certainly in a hurry because about nine months later their first child, George Blackburn Robinson, was born in Leake, about eight miles to the north-east of Boston. At the usual two yearly intervals, George was followed by Harriet and Anne Maria. The 1851 census describes Christopher as a 'cottager of 4½ acres' and his eldest child as his 'son in law'. It is most curious that George's parents chose to highlight that their first born had been conceived out of wedlock. Christopher and Maria completed their family with Charles Christopher, Edward and Eliza Mary born between 1851 and 1856.

The 1861 census lists Harriet Robinson, dairy maid, and Rebecca Howard, housemaid, servants to a farmer and his family at Church End, Leake, adjacent to the Vicarage House. A decade later, Rebecca's younger sister, Ann Howard, was housemaid to the Vicar of Leake at the same Vicarage House so the Robinson and Howard families were clearly well acquainted.

In 1871 Charles Christopher Robinson was nineteen and a coal salesman who was not as tied to the land as his forefathers. Indeed, from Old Leake the Great Northern Railway took him to Boston and then Lincoln, and from there, the Great Central Railway took him on to Sheffield. Of course, migration of the rural population to the industrial cities was rife in the second half of the nineteenth century but Charles had a good reason to choose Sheffield as his destination.

Charles' first cousin, Edward, the oldest child of Thomas and Hannah Robinson of Miningsby, arrived in Westgate, Wakefield, in the year that Charles was born. Five years later Edward married Mary Faulks at St. Paul's Church in Sheffield and their large family was born in Sheffield between 1858 and 1872. Thus, Charles arrived in Sheffield as his cousin and his wife had completed their family.

Edward entered the cutlery trade as a commercial traveller and dealer in plated wares. None of his seven children married and the last survivors, the sisters Eddie and Rose, retired school mistresses, died at 42 Slate Street, Sheffield, in 1945.

Upon arrival in the steel city, Charles sought Christian fellowship in a Primitive Methodist chapel with little success but then he found what he was looking for in Grimesthorpe United Methodist Church, known as Hunsley Street chapel, which had opened in 1868.

A machine worker in the steel industry, in 1875, Charles returned to Leake where he married Ann Howard. The couples' first child, Annie Mary, was born in

February 1876 at 10 Moss Street, close to Hunsley Street chapel, and christened in May at St. Thomas' Church, Brightside. By 1879 the family had crossed the road to 9 Moss Street where Charles William was born in January 1881. Tragically, the little lad died of bronchitis in the following October. Less than three years later, on 7th July 1884, Charles and Ann completed their family with the birth of William Henry Robinson, known to most as Willie.

Due to the lack of documentary evidence, it can only be assumed that Willie received his early education at the Grimesthorpe schools. During that time his father was more often out of work than in so Charles decided to open a shop. Both 35 Carwood Road and later 114-116 Sutherland Road grocery and provision shops were found from advertisements in the Sheffield press. The latter shop was most impressive and in about 1898 a photograph was taken of the family outside it with Willie in the doorway.

Having exhibited an aptitude for learning, Willie completed his formal school education at the age of fourteen and became a pupil teacher. Whilst attending the Pupil Teachers' Centre in Holly Street, which opened in 1899, Willie grew a moustache to distinguish himself from his pupils. Then, at the age of only eighteen, in 1902, he started to contribute articles to the *Teacher's Aid* journal. During the summer of that year Willie took a Physiography examination at the Pupil Teachers' Centre. A fellow candidate, who also took the Model Drawing exam, was a young lady called Edith Craddock.

Edith was the first child of Joseph Craddock, a Midland Railway engineman and his wife, Kate, of 65 Hunsley Street. Edith sat the Brightside Board School King's Scholarship exam in 1903 and taught at Wincobank School. Then, in the summer of 1904, she was transferred to Carlisle Street but was sent to Newhall Junior School instead! In July 1905 both Edith and Willie took time off to sit for their Board of Education Certificate exam. Edith returned to Newhall and Hunsley Street chapel Sunday School where she was the primary department superintendent and the chapel organist for many years.

Willie commenced his teaching career in 1903 at Attercliffe Boys' in Baldwin Street, quickly followed by Park Council Boys' in Norwich Street and Grimesthorpe Council Boys' in Earl Marshal Road.

In September 1906 he entered Sheffield Training College in Collegiate Crescent that had opened only in the previous October in the buildings of the former Royal Grammar School. During Willie's year at the new institution he would have witnessed the official opening, established himself as the Club President and gained the College Certificate: excellence in practical teaching, distinction in Education and English and studied the Advanced Course in English. He also studied English and European History, English Language and Literature at Sheffield University.

In 1907 Willie recommenced teaching at Salmon Pastures Council Senior Mixed in Warren Street and the following year he moved with his family to 266 Ellesmere Road. The Sheffield press provides an interesting insight into Willie's social life at the time since he was then the organiser and renovation secretary at Hunsley Street chapel. In March 1909 a three-day bazaar was held with the objective of raising £150. Charles Wardlow, a steel manufacturer, opened proceedings with the down-beat utterance that 'If there is any slumdom in Sheffield it is at Grimesthorpe'. Indeed, the Craddock family had left Hunsley Street for a newly built house in Earl Marshal Road only the previous year. Kate Craddock and her elder daughter Edith helped tend the Ladies' Congregational Stall whilst Willie's sister, Annie, and Edith's sister, Nellie Craddock, tended the Crockery Stall. Edith's brother, Ernest Craddock, his friend Harry Alvey and others manned the Bazaar Room Entertainments. In June of the following year Willie, as the chapel financial secretary, declared that they had wiped out the large debt. He was also the organising secretary of the chapel Young Peoples's Union of more than fifty members.

In March 1910 Willie joined Newhall Council Senior Mixed in Sanderson Street where Edith was on the staff of the Junior School. Perhaps they felt that fate had intervened and that they were destined to spend the rest of their lives together.

Chapter Two

Author & Father

Willie returned to Grimesthorpe Council Boys' school in Earl Marshal Road in August 1911.

That year he took a special course in Experimental Psychology and Research at Sheffield University and in October he attended the opening of a hall of residence for male students of the Sheffield Training College at Southbourne, 37 Clarkhouse Road. His involvement with the college was such that Willie was appointed the first president of the Sheffield Old Crescenters' Association of about a hundred members. At a social gathering at the college in November, at which the principal, Valentine Ward Pearson, was present, Willie proposed a vote of thanks to the artists.

As previously stated, Willie started to contribute articles to the *Teacher's Aid* journal in 1902. Having also written for the *Teachers' Times* during 1907 and 1908, Willie wrote to the editors of both journals to ask their permission to publish the combined articles in the form of a book. (The editor of the *Teachers' Aid* was J.H. Yoxall who was to be a prominent figure in Willie's professional life.) This was how *The Teachers' ABC* by W.H. Robinson, 'Being ordinary thoughts of an ordinary teacher in an ordinary schoolroom...' came to be published by the Sheffield Independent Press in 1911 (priced at 6d). Perhaps the most important point to emerge from Willie's words of wisdom was to instil in the minds of the young the desire to continue their education after their formal schooling had ended.

Willie clearly enjoyed writing to the press as a means of getting his ideas across. Now a published author, in March 1912, Willie had three full columns of the *Sheffield Daily Telegraph* to tackle the subject of the *Responsibility of Parents*. These were - 1. *Co-partnership in Child Life* referring to the care and education of children, 2. *Uses of Compulsion*, the cleanliness of children and 3. *The Application of Theory*, proposing a Children's Court. Willie was perhaps also clarifying his thoughts in preparation for his future married life with Edith Craddock.

Their wedding took place at Hunsley Street chapel on Wednesday, 29th May 1912. The Rev. V.W. Pearson, first principal of the Sheffield Training College, performed the ceremony, assisted by the Rev. W.H. Brookes of Pye Bank chapel. Bert Unwin was the best man and Bert's sweetheart, Nellie Craddock, and Willie's sister, Annie, were the bridesmaids. Since Earl Marshal Road was a private road belonging to the Duke of Norfolk's estate, Willie had to get permission from the Duke's agent to have the five-bar gate situated halfway along the road opened to allow the wedding party to pass. After the ceremony, guests were entertained at the bride's home at 407 Earl Marshal Road where the newlyweds received gifts from family, friends and Newhall and Grimesthorpe schools. The wedding photograph taken in the back garden is noteworthy for the solemn expressions of the day and the central and dominant position of Willie's sister. The couple then departed for their honeymoon in Derbyshire.

Willie had been elected vice-president of the Sheffield Class Teachers' Association at a meeting at Bow Street schools in July 1911. A year later he was elected president and nominated to be one of four Sheffield delegates to attend the National Federation of Class Teachers' conference in Merthyr in September. Earlier that month, Willie, in his new office, provided words of welcome to 116 new teachers at a reception and dance at the Cutlers' Hall.

Early in 1913 Willie acted as Charitable Purposes Committee secretary to the National Union Teachers' (NUT) Benevolent & Orphan Funds. It is believed that during that year Willie and Edith first met Mr. Swart of Amsterdam at Darley Dale, the Derbyshire home of Edith's aunt Susan Milner and her family. This was the beginning of a very long friendship between the Robinson and Swart families.

For Willie 1914 got off to a bad start when he was absent from Grimesthorpe school for a fortnight due to flu. In February, as secretary of the Sheffield Teachers' Association (STA), he thanked the president for proposing a resolution expressing sympathy with Hertfordshire teachers who were trying to secure a reasonable scale of salaries. Since the STA was the Sheffield branch of the NUT, Willie was elected one of ten Sheffield delegates to attend the NUT conference at Lowestoft where the subject of sex education was on the agenda.

In a column of the *Sheffield Daily Independent* in July Willie compared the success of the King Edward VII School in Sheffield with that of the more modest attainments of the elementary schools. He said that the former provided the 2% to fill the good employment positions but the remaining 98% also needed training to be decent citizens and he called for more elementary school teachers.

Upon the outbreak of war in August the teachers' organisations suspended their annual conferences. Willie transferred to Carbrook Senior Boys' on Attercliffe Common and in December he was elected a committee member of the STA.

At their rented home, 101 Scott Road, Willie and Edith's son was born on 30th March 1915 and named Howard after his paternal grandmother's maiden surname. Willie's best man, Bert Unwin, a steel annealer, then lived with them so it must have been with some relief when he married Nellie Craddock in July and the newlyweds set up home at 51 Idsworth Road. The couple was married at Hunsley Street chapel with May Rideout one of the bridesmaids. To his great disappointment, May's young man, Ernest Craddock was on active service with the Queen's Own Yorkshire Dragoons on the continent and so was unable to attend his sister's wedding.

In September Willie was one of nine Sheffield delegates to the National Federation of Class Teachers' annual congress at Birmingham where the shortage of labour and the employment of children under the age of fourteen were discussed.

In March 1916 conscription for single men aged between 18 and 41 was introduced followed in May by that for married men in the same age range. Willie, who was then in his thirty-second year, was not conscripted due to his misshapen feet for which he required specially made shoes. That April Willie attended an NUT special two-day conference in the Pavilion in Buxton where problems in education arising from the war were discussed.

1917 was a good year for the Robinson families when Willie was able to buy both his parents' house, 266 Ellesmere Road, and the house next door, no. 268, for his own young family. A ground floor connection was made between the houses and it is believed that Willie charged his parents a 'peppercorn rent' for their general store in their front room which was eventually taken over by his sister.

Chapter Three

Sheffield Federated Education Association & the Ilond

The Sheffield Teachers' Association (STA) Education Campaign Committee which was formed in 1913 was suspended due to the war but resumed in the summer of 1917 with the purpose of supporting Fisher's Education Bill. Willie, as a member of the committee, was brimming with ideas of how a sound system of national education could be achieved.

The eighth annual meeting of the Sheffield Class Teachers' Association held at the Hasland Adult School in October 1917 discussed the German educational system. This was deemed to be overly materialistic and lacked spirituality. During the following month Willie presented a lecture entitled 'The Highway of Knowledge' to the Theosophical Society at St. Paul's Parade.

In February 1918 Willie, as secretary of the STA, was due to attend the conference in Cambridge at Easter, and in March he was again president of the Sheffield Class Teachers' Association. Then, by the spring, Willie had formed his very own organisation – the Sheffield Federated Education Association (SFEA).

The SFEA was the first organisation of its kind in the country. Its primary role was to act as an intermediary between the educational authorities and other interested bodies. It would thus sound public opinion and provide speakers on all aspects of education. There was also a bureau of information on educational subjects without pandering to any creed and politics.

At a meeting at the Central School in Leopold Street at the beginning of June it was declared that the SFEA was founded 'to secure for Sheffield the best possible system of education'. J.W. Iliffe, the headmaster of the Central School, was appointed president. Willie, as the secretary, coordinated the contacting of over seven hundred Sheffield organisations and, of those, fifty were invited to be affiliated to the SFEA. As would be expected, not every organisation was keen and a notable rejection came from the Union of Clerks.

Later that month Willie attended the Yorkshire Federation of Class Teachers' Associations conference at Leeds where he was elected vice-president. He was also nominated a Yorkshire candidate for the Federal Council of Class Teachers and for the executive of the NUT. As if he was not busy enough, Willie transferred to Wincobank Senior Mixed School in Newman Road.

With the school leaving age raised to fourteen, Willie contributed a column in the *Sheffield Daily Independent* concerning the implications of the new Education Act on Sheffield. He said that it was time to stop talking in general terms and to state what was to be done. A few days later J.W. Iliffe presided at the quarterly council of the SFEA. He welcomed the Education Act as an advance towards establishing a national system of education.

In October Willie attended the National Federation of Class Teachers' conference in London in his capacity as president of the Sheffield Class Teachers' Association and vice-president of the Yorkshire Federation of Class Teachers. There he was elected a Yorkshire member of the National Federation Council and adopted as a Federation candidate for the NUT executive. The last was apparently endorsed at a STA meeting in December. Then, just before Christmas, Willie as SFEA honorary secretary, wrote to the Sheffield press concerning 'Educational Needs', 'School Accommodation' and highlighting the pressure on existing school buildings.

The spring of 1919 brought mixed fortunes for Willie when he was invited to address Blackpool teachers on the subject of backwardness in children but then he failed to be elected to the executive at the NUT annual conference at the Town Hall in Cheltenham. That May he transferred to Huntsman's Gardens Senior Mixed School in Bodmin Street and gave a talk on 'Education and the Law of Liberty' at Victoria Hall.

In June Willie was elected president of the Yorkshire Federation of Class Teachers and the SFEA held its first annual meeting at the Boys' Central Secondary School. A vice-president, William Sinclair, reported that there were then nearly fifty affiliated organisations of trade unions, adult schools, friendly societies etc. J.W Iliffe resigned his position as president due to the pressure of his other activities but agreed to be one of the six vice-presidents. The presidential position was filled by the Rev. F. D. Tranter. Willie, as honorary secretary contributed a series of memoranda on educational movements.

The crowning achievement of the SFEA was probably the council meeting at Victoria Hall in September where the Rt. Hon. H.A.L. Fisher MP, President of the Board of Education, spoke on the 1918 Education Act. The vice-chancellor of Sheffield University, Dr. William Ripper, presided and introduced Dr. Percival Sharp, Sheffield's new Director of Education. Willie's contribution was as editor of a SFEA special report on music, physical training and nursery schools. He cannot have been present the whole time since that same day he also attended the National Federation of Class Teachers' annual conference at Liverpool. As president of the Yorkshire Federation of Class Teachers' Associations he was elected a Yorkshire member of the Federation Council.

Around the turn of the year Willie attended two STA meetings at the Girls' Central Secondary School. At the one, in December, he was elected to the committee for 1920 and nominated for the NUT executive. At the other, in February, he joined the West Yorkshire County Association council for that year. At a SFEA meeting at the end of that month the new Education Act was discussed with the Sheffield Education Committee chairman and the Director of Education.

Willie and Edith completed their family with the birth of Margaret, always known as Peggy, who was born at 268 Ellesmere Road on 14th March 1920. Her brother, Howard, remembered that it was snowy day. Peggy was christened on 18th April at Hunsley Street chapel.

At the NUT Golden Jubilee conference later that month at Margate, Willie once again failed to be elected to the executive.

Wednesday, 2nd June was a busy day for Willie. In the morning he was one of four Huntsman's Gardens staff in charge of 185 Standard 6, 7, & 8 pupils taken to view the Shackleton Antarctic Exhibition at Sheffield's Albert Hall. In the afternoon he arrived in time to appear in the back row of a family group photograph which was taken at The Tower dance hall on Burngreave Road. The occasion was the wedding reception of Edith's brother, Ernest Craddock, to May Rideout.

A few weeks later, Edith, with Peggy in the pram, collected Howard from Firs Hill School. Then, they and Edith's parents, Joseph and Kate Craddock, picnicked a few score yards away on the edge of Roe Wood with Sylvia Kennedy, a relative visiting from Melbourne in Australia.

Henry Caldwell Cook's book *The Play Way, An Essay in Educational Method* was published in 1917. Cook reasoned that 'the natural means of study in youth is play' and that this could be harnessed to stimulate the joy of learning. The book's frontispiece is a colourful depiction of an imaginary island or Ilond designed to intrigue and inspire the young reader. (And presumably, challenge the concept of the rigidity of spelling.)

Willie was intrigued by Cook's thesis and in April 1920, with his headmaster's approval, started to introduce these ideas into the curriculum of his Standard 8 Boys at Huntsman's Gardens School. Standard 8 was the final year for pupils at elementary school and, as such, on the verge of their working life, they could be the most difficult pupils to reach.

Having instituted a class parliament, started a debating society and organised exhibitions, Willie also took his pupils on works' visits. He divided his class into six 'tribes' - Athletes, Invincibles, Spartans, Trojans, Undaunted and Stoics. Guided by worksheets, gradually the boys (and later, girls) took to the idea of working independently for their own satisfaction and for the benefit of their tribe. Their Ilond motto 'The best is nearly good enough for us' was designed to encourage the pupils to aim high.

In July Willie was in charge of sixteen Standard 8 boys on a visit to Norfolk Steel Works. At the end of the year the Government Inspector was apparently 'very much impressed' with the Ilond.

Chapter Four

Presentations & Sheffield Education Week

At the Sheffield Federated Education Association's (SFEA) second annual meeting in the summer of 1920, Willie, as secretary, announced that the last year's annual report had created world-wide interest with requests coming from Australia, New Zealand and the USA. In Sheffield however, they were short of 120 teachers and a hundred classes lacked a good teacher.

On 1st September Willie registered as a teacher with the Teachers Registration Council and was admitted as a member of the Royal Society of Teachers. Later that month at the National Federation of Class Teachers' conference at Ipswich the reorganisation of the whole primary school system was urged. In November Willie delivered a lecture at the Sheffield Co-operative Men's Guild on 'Modern views on Education'. He said that the 'high rates are not due to high expenditure on education. The rate for elementary education in Sheffield had not increased in the same proportions as the other rates in the past ten years'.

In January 1921 the Sheffield press published Willie's letter on 'The Cost of Education'. He pointed out that in the year 1913-14 10% of national revenue was spent on education but for 1920-21 this had dropped to only 5% with unprecedented demand for secondary education and crowded universities. Two months later the same papers published joint letters (with B. Topliss) on the 'Value of Publicity in Education' and 'Should the Babies Go to School?' The SFEA president, the Rev. Tranter, presided at the Nether School to report on protests against economy and the Northampton Education Week. The latter subject initiated a special meeting of the SFEA at Bow Street Council School to suggest organising a Sheffield Education Week in October. To this end, Willie and the Rev. Tranter's joint letter to the Sheffield press was published in early May informing the public about the work of the SFEA and proposing 'A Sheffield Education Week'. Unfortunately, that did not happen in 1921 but the seed had been sown.

At the National Federation of Class Teachers' annual conference at Portsmouth in September, Willie was elected vice-president with more votes than the two opposition candidates combined. He urged for better conditions in the schools and that pupils should be encouraged to remain at school until they had secured a job.

The following month, to the Sheffield & Ecclesall Co-op Men's Guild, Willie called for more money to be spent on education and pointed out that Sheffield spent less than the national average. This culminated in a SFEA conference on 'Educational Efficiency' held at the Mappin Hall of the University of Sheffield in March 1922. Presided over by Sir William Clegg, Willie's address stated that the average family spent three times more on alcohol, tobacco and entertainments as they did on education.

Three months later at the SFEA's third annual conference Sir William Henry Hadow, vice-chancellor of the University of Sheffield, was elected president, George Green became the treasurer and Willie remained the secretary.

The 28th annual conference of the National Federation of Class Teachers' was held in the Firth Hall of the University of Sheffield in September. Delegates were welcomed by the Lord Mayor, Alderman Charles Simpson, and chairman of the Education Committee, Sir William Clegg. Willie, the founder and secretary of the SFEA, was installed as the new president and addressed the conference on the subject of salaries and efficiency. He emphasised that 'This conference declares its strong opposition to any reduction of educational facilities'. At a reception in the ballroom of the Town Hall, Willie thanked the Lord Mayor and the Lady Mayoress and the artists for their entertainment. Willie and Edith were presented with a mahogany case of fish knives. Then, little Peggy Robinson, aged just two and half, presented Miss Aston, the outgoing president, with a case of tea knives and a silver manicure set.

Presentations were also the order of a day in December when Willie, in his new office as president, attended a memorial service at the Cathedral for Miss Isabel Cleghorn, the first female president of both the STA and of the NUT. Miss Cleghorn had been head of the girls' department of Heeley Bank School from 1880 to 1918.

In March 1923 Willie gave a SFEA address to the Free Churchmen at Grimesthorpe presenting a public petition against the reduction of educational facilities. When the Sheffield newspapers refused to sympathise with the teachers, Willie spent £100 on advertisements to state the teachers' case. Two of those, *The Children's Charter* and *The Kiddies and their future* appeared in the *Sheffield Independent* on 12th and 13th March respectively appealing for additional signatures for the petition. On 15th March it was announced that 13,093 signatures had been collected. Only then did the City Council reverse their economic proposal.

As the president of the National Federation of Class Teachers, Willie attended the Durham County Union of Federations annual meeting at Durham in June. In his address *Public Opinion and Education*, he asked the question – 'Was any child not capable of profiting by education?' emphasising again that five times as much was spent on drink as on education.

For Willie and Edith the years 1923 to 1925 were saddened by four deaths in their families.

After their wartime wedding, nearly eight years passed before Bert and Nellie Unwin expected their first child. When complications developed, Nellie moved back to the Craddock residence at 407 Earl Marshal Road where Edith was on hand to help care for her sister. Tragically, little Betty Unwin, lived only the last two days of June 1923 before succumbing to a cerebral haemorrhage. With Nellie an invalid and her father ailing, Edith, Howard and Peggy moved to 407 to assist Edith's mother. Joseph Craddock died on 6th May 1924 aged seventy-six and Nellie died on 30th June just thirty-four, and as if to add to the tragedy, precisely a year to the day after the death of her baby daughter.

The following year, Willie's father, Charles Robinson died aged seventy-three of liver cancer.

In September 1923, Willie, as the out-going president of the National Federation of Class Teachers, told the conference in Birmingham that those most critical of the teachers knew least about their work. He then read an extract from a letter by the chairman of the Cammel Laird steel company who said 'Speaking very broadly, I do not much care what a boy learns so long as he learns how to learn'. Willie very much concurred with his statement.

The following month, Willie presided at the Cutlers' Hall as vice-president of the STA. This he followed up with letters to the press concerning improving communications between teachers and the Education Committees, teachers' pensions and the Burnham Scale of salaries. This reached fruition at the November conference of Sheffield Education Committee representatives with a deputation of Sheffield teachers to discuss the recent examination in elementary schools.

In December it was announced that Willie would be the STA president for 1924. It was during that year that the Association took the Sheffield Corporation to the High Court. The legal action concerned the heads – Joe Francis Sadler of St. Jude's School, Moorfields and Rose Dyson of St. George's Church of England School – who were dismissed when they refused to accept less than the agreed Burnham salary. Success in the High Court boded well for Willie's presidential year in office. His address - *Success and joint control of Schools* was presented at the Girls' Secondary School in February 1924.

The Ilond, a country in the clouds of a child's imagination, continued to inspire Standard 8 pupils at Huntsman's Gardens School. By April 1924 Willie had divided his class into five tribes – Invincibles, Lionhearts, Olympians, Neapolitans and Dreadnoughts – the initial letters of which spell Ilond. Willie was 'chums' with his boys but he always took the role of the older brother. By this means his quiet, yet firm handling of sixty lads impressed his headmaster who described his ability in glowing terms. Prof. John Adams of London University was also impressed and said that Willie obviously had a special gift for dealing with boys at a most critical age. The litmus test during the depressed 1920s was when all sixty boys obtained employment and favourable comments were received from employers.

In July, Hunsley Street chapel bid a fond farewell to the Rev. Albert Hearn who had been the minister since 1918. He and his wife were presented with a silver-plated tea service and four-year-old Peggy Robinson gave Mrs. Hearn a bouquet.

At the National Federation of Class Teachers' conference at Stratford Town Hall in September there was a call for the abolition of large classes in the elementary schools. It was declared that education was not a charity. It was an insurance against future social inefficiency.

Three years after the SFEA first proposed the idea of a Sheffield Education Week, the event materialised during the week of 16th to 22nd November 1924. Willie was the Publicity Committee secretary and read the lesson in the Cathedral. He also asked some of his boys at Huntsman's Gardens School to give a demonstration of the Ilond. At the STA half-century annual general meeting in February 1925, Willie, as out-going president, said that the Sheffield Education Week had been very successful. He also paid tribute to the late Sir James Henry Yoxall who had been general secretary of the NUT from 1892 to 1924.

With impeccable timing, Willie regained his presidential title a few days later when he was installed as president of the West Yorkshire County Association (WYCA) at the Grand Hotel. To that organisation, which was affiliated to the NUT, Willie addressed the annual conference of the subject of 'Waste in Education'. To that end he suggested that schools should adopt two or three streams to cater for pupils of differing ability. Willie supported this during April with the publication of his WYCA memo on *A National System of Education.*

At the WYCA conference in Leeds in May, Willie said that care should be taken to compare those teachers who taught most to those who taught best. He concluded that what was required was the best teachers for primary schools, more provision for older pupils and assessment by work rather than by exams.

Willie built on those points to the same organisation at Ilkley in July and wrote to the *Sheffield Daily Telegraph* on the subject of *Teachers and Older Pupils*. In the latter letter he had to explain that, in deference to his chief, he was not in fact the headmaster of Huntsman's Gardens School.

Willie's term as president of the WYCA ended in March 1926 at the annual conference at the Hotel Metropole in Leeds. There he presented *A National System of Education* from the memo written during the previous year. He outlined a scheme to ensure that every child had a secondary education from the age of eleven. He also pitied the bright child who was rushed to the top class – for Willie was sure they would lose much in the process.

As the WYCA representative, Willie attended the STA conference at Margate at Easter and was one of twelve Sheffield representatives at the NUT annual conference at Portsmouth.

By that summer the Ilond tribes at Huntsman's Gardens had been brought back home by being called Britons, Saxons, Normans and Danes. A debate was organised between Standard 8B2 and Standard 8B3 by pitting the Team System against the Ilond System. Apparently, Willie held the Ilond president, Douglas North, in high esteem as he displayed his photograph above his desk.

That year's Hadow Report recommended raising the school leaving age to fifteen and replacing the elementary, all-age, schools with primary and secondary schools. At this important juncture, in January 1927, Willie succeeded C.W. Cowen as editor of *The Hallamshire Teacher*, the journal of the STA. The following month he attended the STA annual conference and was nominated one of thirteen representatives for the NUT conference in Margate and one of eleven for the WYCA conference.

At the WYCA annual conference at the Victory Hotel at Leeds Willie submitted a resolution that a pupil's capability should not be judged on exam results alone. He said 'offer them the best in literature, science and the arts – they will reject much but what they do retain they will retain for life'. Willie's and other comments resulted in stories in the press such as – *Teachers who would abolish exams*.

Chapter Five

A Rail Crash & Pipworth Road

On 14th May 1927 Willie returned to Sheffield on the Edinburgh to London express in the company of T.E. Hepworth. They were respectively vice-president and president of the STA and had just attended the NUT conference in Leeds.

At about 4-20pm the pair were just finishing their tea in the dining car when the slowing train was hit by a locomotive which was reversing from a branch line at Sheffield LMS station. A buffer on the locomotive ripped through the wooden side of the dining car 'like an iron claw' causing a window to fall on Willie and Mr. Hepworth. In total, a dozen of the dining car's occupants were injured but only two were detained in hospital. Willie was cut about his scalp and a piece of glass just missed an artery in his neck. Hepworth was injured in his cheek and hand. Both men were bandaged on the platform by ambulance personnel but declined to go to hospital. Despite the stoicism recorded by the press, Willie took two weeks off from Huntsman's Gardens School whilst he recovered from his cuts and bruises.

Building on the success of the first Sheffield Education Week in 1924, in the summer of 1927, Willie was the teaching profession representative and Publicity Committee secretary for that year's Education Week. In the latter role, Willie was placed in charge of producing the handbook, posters and handbills.

Sheffield Education Week ran from 8th to 15th October 1927 and, largely due to Willie's efforts, it was stated that 'the Sheffield papers have given greater support to the Education Week than has been the case in other towns'. Hailed as 'the Publicity Expert of the Sheffield Education World', Willie addressed a meeting at Nether Chapel on the success of the Education Week. Perhaps the activity of the year caught up with Willie when, just before Christmas, he took three weeks off from Huntsman's Gardens School due to sciatica and neuritis.

The spring of 1928 brought Willie renewed vigour when he again ran for the NUT executive. His election poster proclaimed that he was 'The only candidate who is a class teacher' and that he was backed by both the president and vice-president of the Yorkshire Federation of Class Teachers.

Willie became one of the three Yorkshire members of the executive at the annual conference at the Guildhall, Cambridge in April when it was declared that he was the first assistant master to be elected for many years. W.W. Hill was installed as president of the NUT and C.W. Cowen as vice-president.

Closer to home, that same month, a new classroom was opened at Hunsley Street chapel to coincide with the Diamond Jubilee year. Willie was secretary of Trustees and Teachers' Training Class leader.

At the end of September Willie attended the National Federation of Class Teachers' annual conference at Bradford. The president, Ralph Morley, in criticising the Hadow Report, opposed breaking education at the age of eleven and the introduction of grammar, modern and senior secondary schools. Willie seconded the proposal that they wanted to raise the school leaving age to fifteen in 1933, reduce class sizes and establish free secondary education for all.

During Willie's term as president of the Sheffield Class Teachers' Association (1928-9) he commented on the President of the Board of Education's preface to the *Handbook of Education for Industry and Commerce*.

The New Year of 1929 for Willie brought election as honorary secretary of the National Federation of Class Teachers, a letter in the *Sheffield Independent* concerning the importance of scholarships to entry to secondary schools and, unfortunately, illness. A fortnight's absence from school due to flu and two visits to a specialist culminated in surgical treatment for an undisclosed condition on 22nd March.

Eight days later, Willie travelled to North Wales for the 59th NUT annual conference at the Pier Pavilion at Llandudno. There, where David Lloyd George MP spoke to the assembly, C.W. Cowen was installed as president and Willie moved a resolution to call upon local authorities to provide playing fields and open spaces.

Elected a member of the Burnham Committee in May, two months later Willie took the train down to London to act in that capacity. There, on the House of Commons terrace on a hot July afternoon, Willie, Ralph Morley MP, W.B. Steer and H.J. Lane worked out the details of the Burnham Basic Scale for teachers' salaries.

Now associated with the decision makers in education, Willie believed that he deserved a headship. To this end he produced a seven page pamphlet detailing his academic, teaching experience, ability and general experience etc. and containing numerous references from former and current headmasters and academics. Unfortunately, it was to no avail and Willie only succeeded in securing another assistant master position. Willie reluctantly closed down the Ilond system at Huntsman's Gardens and on 25th July he left the school.

That summer, Willie and his family took their holiday in Bridlington. Peggy recalled the huge black case that was filled with clothing and some food that was then despatched by rail 'luggage in advance' to their destination. Willie was then able to use his NUT railway concession to convey both himself and his family. That year, Willie, Edith, Howard and Peggy, the children then being fourteen and nine respectively, were accompanied by Stanley and Joan Craddock, eight and five years old, since their mother, May, was then expecting her third child.

On 26th August 1929 Willie joined the staff of Pipworth Road Council Senior Mixed School on Prince of Wales Road.

After the series of solid but very Victorian Board schools of his career to date, the first modern school of its type in Sheffield offered a refreshing change of environment. Under the headmaster A.E. Hanney, Willie was placed in charge of the twenty-two boys and eleven girls of Form III – the top form. A month into his new job he took his form to the 'Save the Countryside Exhibition' at the Cutlers' Hall.

The very next day Willie was in Assembly Rooms at Derby attending the National Federation of Class Teachers' annual conference. Ralph Morley MP, the retiring president, proposed and Willie seconded a motion that the word 'elementary' should be purged from educational circles. The conference welcomed the raising of the school leaving age to fifteen in 1931.

Back in Sheffield, the Rt. Hon. Sir Charles Trevelyan PC MP, president of the Board of Trade, officially opened four schools on 3rd October including Pipworth Road. Presumably reflecting the higher school leaving age, by April 1930 Willie was in charge of Form IVb – equal top form. Also that month, Willie was re-elected a member of the Burnham Committee Teachers' Panel.

1931 got off to a bad start for Willie when he took a fortnight in February off due to a severe cold and laryngitis.

Willie was one of eleven Sheffield representatives who attended the NUT annual conference at the Floral Hall, Britannia Pier in Yarmouth at the beginning of April. In the presence of the Duke and Duchess of York, C.W. Cowen presided over the installation of the new president. There was a resolution to raise the school leaving age to fifteen and limit class sizes to forty. At the end of the month, Willie was again elected to the NUT executive and the Burnham Committee to negotiate teachers' salaries.

After attending a fortnight Board of Education course at Cambridge in July, two months later, Willie moved the first resolution at the STA meeting at Victoria Hall to oppose any proposal that would impair the efficiency of the State schools.

Chapter Six

Sharrow Lane Head & two Jubilees

Howard maintained that his father's progressive ideas and his union activities impeded his advancement to a headship. Certainly, the surviving school log books record the large number of days he took off work in order to attend union meetings around the country. Despite that, on 24th September 1931 it was announced in the Sheffield press that Willie had been appointed headmaster of Sharrow Lane Council Boys' School in South View Road.

The school's first head had been Sir James Henry Yoxall who was later secretary of the NUT and whose portrait hung in the school hall. He was succeeded by Daniel Maidment, Frederick William Allen and Sydney Arthur Howe until ill-health compelled the last named to retire. On 30th September Willie left Pipworth Road and the following month he became the fifth headmaster of Sharrow Lane.

Despite his new responsibilities, in March 1932 Willie was re-elected to the NUT executive and he attended the conference at Folkestone. There he proposed that the proper measure was of the mental qualities of the child and that progression from primary to secondary school should be made when the child was ready.

Three days before Christmas, Willie's mother-in-law, Kate Craddock, died at their home at 268 Ellesmere Road where Edith had cared for her bedridden mother. Seventeen-year-old Howard cycled to Hunsley Street to break the news to his grandmother's sister, Tilly Merrick, and her family who lived almost opposite the chapel and to his uncle, Bert Unwin, at Cammel Laird steel works.

In April 1933 Willie attended the NUT conference at Aberystwyth where he said that children in many schools worked in conditions which would not satisfy the Factory Acts.

Back in Sheffield, in December, Willie presided over a tribute to Miss Emily Morgan, head of Sharrow Lane Girls' and Junior Mixed School after her forty years of service.

In February 1934, Willie joined a STA deputation to the House of Commons where they were received by all seven of the Sheffield MPs. As members of the Yorkshire Executive, they pleaded their case for an early restoration of the 10% salary cut as a preliminary to re-opening discussion of the Burnham Scale. The following month Willie was one of four candidates vying for three places on the NUT Yorkshire Executive. That achieved, he then attended the NUT conference at the Royal Pavilion in Brighton at Easter.

That summer, during the open day presentation of swimming awards, Willie would have been delighted to hear Sharrow Lane described as one of the most active schools in Sheffield. It was also the only elementary school in the city with an internal telephone system. The exchange was operated by the school prefects with phones in Willie's room, the hall and two classrooms. In addition to the usual academic lessons, a motor car engine was dismantled and re-assembled almost daily in the school's workshop to provide the pupils with knowledge of practical mechanics.

A highlight for the School that July was when twelve-year-old John A. Smith was announced as the top boy in Sheffield for the examination for admittance to secondary school. A photograph was published in the *Sheffield Independent* of Willie shaking John's hand in front of his fellow pupils seated cross-legged in the hall. John was the recipient of the first top scholar's bronze medal to be offered by the Sheffield Old Scholars' Federation.

The annual distribution of certificates and open day in December was attended by the Lord Mayor of Sheffield, Alderman P.J.M. Turner who told the assembly that he had just come from the Hillsborough football ground and that the half-time score between Sheffield Wednesday and Austria was 0-0. The Lady

Mayoress then presented the certificates and Willie reminded them of John Smith's achievement.

In February 1935 Willie was elected vice-president of the Sheffield Head Teachers' Association and in March he attended the 25th annual conference of the Yorkshire Federation of Head Teachers' Associations at the Junior Technical School. At the latter, Willie moved an amendment against using exam results as the basis for scholarships and recommended weight being given to a pupil's school records. He also claimed that teachers did not want the responsibility of deciding careers for pupils.

In May, Sheffield, and indeed the entire British Empire, celebrated King George V and Queen Mary's Silver Jubilee. Each child of school age was presented with a Jubilee medal designed by the Sheffield College of Arts and Crafts.

That summer at the West Yorkshire County Association meeting at the Hotel Metropole in Leeds, Willie suggested that cabinet ministers make radio broadcasts specifically composed to be heard in schools. He claimed that educationists had so far failed to exploit the power of radio and that ministers could use that medium to influence their future electorate.

Sheffield Education Week held between 29th September and 5th October cost £319 13s 10d – nearly £20 overspent! Having spent £90 on advertising, Willie thanked the Sheffield press for their coverage of the event.

In October Alderman E.G. Rowlinson, Sheffield Education Committee chairman, distributed the certificates and medallions at Sharrow Lane School. Mr. H.S. Newton, the Chief Education Officer, said that Willie and his staff were to be congratulated on their progress and the parents on their co-operation with the teachers. Willie was described as one of the most loyal and hard-working headmasters in the City. This was supported in December by the school inspector noting the head's 'enthusiasm and enterprise'.

In January 1936 Willie travelled down to London with C.W. Cowen to attend the opening of the £50,000 extension to the NUT Headquarters at Hamilton House by Lord Onslow, the Burnham Committee chairman.

Having again been re-elected a Yorkshire member of the NUT executive, on that occasion by postal ballot, Willie gave his presidential address to the Sheffield Head Teachers' Association at Carver Street Chapel School in March. He again attacked exams saying that what was needed was not a 'snapshot' but a 'film' of a child's progress.

The NUT conference at the Garrick Theatre at Southport at Easter was attended by six thousand delegates from France, Belgium, Denmark, the Netherlands, Eire as well as this country. At the end of May, Willie was then in Lincoln for the 39th annual conference of the National Association of Head Teachers. He seconded a proposition that infant schools should remain a separate entity.

At the end of June it was proposed that an Old Scholars' Association was formed for the benefit of ex-pupils of the Sharrow Lane schools. This was timed to mark the Golden Jubilee of the School which had opened on 21st February 1887.

Ideas were brought to fruition in October when a re-union social gathering was proposed for 27th February 1937. Willie presided over the proceedings and was elected president of the Association. The vice-president was the current headmistress of the girls' department. The Jubilee was advertised by posters and covered by the Sheffield press. There was an open week at the school and open evening at the evening school. Ex-pupils responded from all over the country and one reply came from Australia. Over a hundred pupils put on a concert of plays and bands that was attended by over two hundred.

Three months after the School's Jubilee, King George VI and Queen Elizabeth were crowned in Westminster Abbey. In celebration of the city's cutlery industry, every boy in Sheffield of school age was presented with a penknife and every girl with a pair of scissors.

Chapter Seven

Redcote & the British Association

After attaining a headship, Willie must have had a growing sense of achievement. However, as Howard and Peggy grew to adulthood, they must have felt that they had out-grown their terrace house at 268 Ellesmere Road. Leaving Willie's mother and sister, Anne and Annie, to tend their provisions shop next door at 266 Ellesmere Road, Willie became the first of his family to own a detached house in Sheffield.

Redcote, 14 Crabtree Lane, in Old Crabtree, was built on a large corner plot in about 1908. It had six bedrooms, a cellar and a detached garage with a room above. It was successively occupied by a chief engineering draughtsman, a steel merchant, a professor of French at Sheffield University and a teacher at Firshill School. The last, Miss Nellie Boothby, died in February 1938 and the Robinsons moved in to Redcote in the spring or early summer. Fitted out with the modern conveniences, Peter Craddock was particularly impressed that his uncle and aunt had a refrigerator!

In April Willie was one of three Yorkshire representatives elected to the NUT executive. Later that month he attended the conference in Margate where he moved an amendment.

Three months later, in an interview by the *Sheffield Daily Independent*, Willie said that 'There are many things more important than the 3Rs which cannot be tested by exams'.

Willie then owned a second-hand Lanchester 9 and, although generally considered to be a poor driver, he managed to convey himself and his family to Tudweiliog, near Nevin, in North Wales for their summer holiday. He, Edith and the eighteen-year-old

Peggy were accompanied by Joan and Peter Craddock, aged fourteen and nine respectively, since their mother was expecting her fourth child.

Joan wrote to her mother that they had had a puncture between Knutsford and Northwich and that two workmen helped them to put on the spare wheel. According to Joan the weather was 'rotten' and they experienced rough weather on the coast. Spending much time in the car, Willie used his considerable ingenuity to entertain the youngsters as they watched the rain clouds pass over. Unfortunately, they punctured again on the way to Caernarvon Castle.

Peter had fond memories of his uncle and the fact that he was very good with children. As a small boy Peter climbed through the 'coal-hole' formed by his uncle's crossed legs and enjoyed his game of bears. The last entailed Willie persuading as many as possible to get on their hands and knees and to ask each in turn if they knew how to play bears. It must have come as a bit of a disappointment to the uninitiated when it turned out that no one, including Willie, knew how to play bears.

The highlight of Willie's professional career was undoubtedly his invitation to address the British Association at Cambridge in August 1938. Apparently, it was an unprecedented honour for the headmaster of an elementary school.

In the Educational Science section, 'Education for a changing society', Willie presented a paper entitled 'Senior Schools'. Willie's speech was summarized in the *Sheffield Telegraph* on 20th August as follows -

> The senior school was the school of the people of England.
>
> The essential function of school in a changing society was to teach pupils the art of self-education and to convince them that education was not a thing of school alone.
>
> The school must be related at all points to the community, and, in the words of the Hadow Committee, "the curriculum has to be thought of in terms of activity and experience rather than of knowledge to be acquired and facts to be stored."

The year from 14 to 15 should be used to consolidate the training which has already been given, by taking into full account the psychology of the adolescents.

They will become the leaders of the school community. They will get their experience of life through the organisation of school activities – sport, societies, dramatic work, etc., and by discussion and attempt at agreement they will learn by experience the basic facts on which our democracy is based and along which it must develop.

They will learn in community life the necessity for patience, persuasion and compromise; that toleration is better than coercion.

This learning through experience will be more important than lessons. It should be an integral part in their education, not something to be squeezed into odd moments left over from education proper.

If we teach them to read and how to find information and if we supplement what they are daily learning from newspapers, cinemas and broadcasting; we must remember that the same facts mean different things to Mussolini, Hitler, Chamberlain and Anthony Eden.

The great need appears to be for the development of a technique by means of which there is developed the active co-operation of the pupil in the work of self-education for life.

This is the implicit aim of all organised education. Only as the pupil understands what it is all about and is led consciously to co-operate in a process of real education for life will the system succeed.

This cannot be left to chance or merely be expected to develop in the right atmosphere but must become the dominant note in the new technique of the senior school.

Chapter Eight

Evacuation & the Blitz

The following months brought closer the terrifying prospect of another world war.

In March 1939, at a meeting at Sharrow Lane School, parents aired their concerns about plans to evacuate their children and pressed for an alternative in the provision of adequate air-raid shelters. Two months later Willie was named as the leader of his school's evacuation party and, in July, Dr. W.J. Ogilvie was placed in charge of the first aid post to be based at the school in the event of war.

In anticipation of an imminent declaration of war, Willie led his school party to Heeley railway station bound for Loughborough conveyed by the London, Midland and Scottish Railway Company. Thus, on 1st September the first train with eight hundred Sheffield schoolchildren formed the vanguard of nine thousand who arrived in Loughborough and were taken to schools and other suitable buildings. There the children were provided with forty-eight hour rations and dispersed to family homes in the district. Householders were paid 10/6 per week for accommodating a single child, 8/6 for further children. In all, 15% of Sheffield school children were sent to Loughborough, Newark and Melton Mowbray.

In mid September the *Sheffield Daily Telegraph* and several newspapers in the Midlands published a letter from Willie. Based at the Education Office on Ashby Road in Loughborough, Willie, as representative of Sheffield Head Teachers in Loughborough, thanked the officials and people of the town for their assistance and help with the huge job of re-locating so many children.

This was the start of the so-called 'Phoney War', when, after a few weeks away from home the children gradually returned to Sheffield. With the closure of the schools, children received 'Home Service' lessons in widely dispersed private homes. Peggy Robinson remembered that for a period a Mr. Johnson taught a form from Firth Park Grammar School in Willie's study over the garage at Redcote.

Sharrow Lane School was then an ARP centre and in November it hosted an air raid drill for nearly sixty personnel of Southern E Group to determine their speed and efficiency. By Christmas 1939 all but two thousand evacuated children had returned to Sheffield.

The Blitz came to Sheffield nearly a year later on the night of 13th December 1940.

Sharrow Lane School received a direct hit killing Harry Doyle, an ARP warden of a similar age to Willie. The central block and the first floor boys' accommodation were demolished and in Willie's words 'The whole of the contents was reduced to fine powder'.

With 174 boys on the roll, some were re-located to Abbeydale, Pomona, St. Matthias' and Hunters Bar schools. At Sharrow Lane there was one room for the Junior Department, room for a dozen in their hall and forty spaces in the Handicraft Centre. Willie secured the hall of the Institute for the Blind and the Training College Gym and, after cleaning up the staff room, he brought an electric fire from home. There his staff of seven could brew a pot of tea and enjoy a smoke. At this difficult time, Willie told Peggy that 'no matter how hard the winter, the roses will come again in the spring'.

For Willie, 'the roses' provided the opportunity to 'experiment in our own procedures'. He could now put into practice much of which he had been theorising and experimenting with for years. His staff naturally looked to him for leadership but, with limited resources he could offer them little but to suggest that they were now not teachers but educators. Willie cared not a fig what they taught in their lessons but what the pupils could gain from their guidance. Then, in Willie's words the 'pennies dropped'. Both teachers and pupils began to realise that he expected them to create an environment rather than to teach and be taught. He asked his staff to facilitate their pupil's education through 'activity and experience' and by suggesting that there was 'a world of difference between hard work and efficient work'. Willie used the recent fall of France as an example of the closed minded thinking that he wanted put aside. In Willie's words-

There was quite a number of 'brass-hats' who were so busy soldiering that they really hadn't time to be bothered about fancy ideas concerning blitzkriegs and tanks and aeroplanes, even after the war had started, and how pathetic was the faith in Weygand and Gamelin and the Maginot Line.

Willie referred to this as 'The Maginot mind' and he hoped that his staff would rid themselves of this complex. Hydroponics – growing plants without soil – Willie cited as a good example of what he wanted to achieve.

One of Willie's assistant masters intentionally left a gardening magazine open at a page displaying an advertisement for a Hydroponics kit. On entering the classroom a group of boys found the magazine and were intrigued by what they read. They sent for the kit and, using their considerable ingenuity in wartime Britain, they built the required container, waterproofed it and endeavoured to grow tomato and radish plants without the use of soil. When the radishes developed a disease, they sent a sample to a gardening journal and, on receiving a reply, the boys acted on the advice. Although, today it seems like an everyday matter, it was then a rarity and a delight for thirteen-year-olds to receive a letter addressed to them through the post. The boys had not been told what to do; their master had simply engaged their enthusiasm which, in turn, had boosted their self-confidence and their capacity to self-educate.

After an overnight air raid on Sheffield, Peggy celebrated her twenty-first birthday with a few friends in March 1941.

A month later her grandmother, Anne Robinson, died of bronchitis aged eighty-nine. Willie described his mother as being 'one of the last Puritans' since she made a point of walking to chapel on Sunday. She refused to take the tram and so be the cause of someone else working and handling money on the Sabbath.

Howard had hoped to marry his childhood sweetheart Margaret Melluish in June 1941 but since he couldn't get leave from the army they tied the knot at Hanover Street Methodist Church in Sheffield on 1st November. Peggy and

Margaret's sister, Mary Hines, in dresses designed for June, were the shivering bridesmaids at a reception held at Redcote. The happy couple's first child, David, was born in Sheffield on 4th September 1942. After the war Howard taught at Erith Technical College in which town Christine was born on 7th August 1947.

In July 1941 Willie invited all to an open day at Sharrow Lane. The School then had an allotment at Hutcliffe Wood so that the boys could help to 'Dig for Victory'. They built a shed and greenhouse – all good outside activities – which was just as well because the lack of accommodation meant that forty boys had to be outdoors somewhere including during the winter.

The winter of 1941-2 was severe. Willie found that his fingers were too cold to hold a pen to mark the register and plaster regularly fell from the ceiling onto his lunch. He was almost hit by a falling window frame which perhaps brought back memories of the rail crash in 1927. Both staff and pupils had also to cope without washing facilities and the senior boys' had only limited use of the Infants' Department WCs.

Despite the conditions, the wartime spirit shone through. A good example of this occurred in August 1942 when the firewatchers based at the School complained that their fire buckets had been interfered with. Some of the senior boys took it upon themselves to show that it was not the Sharrow Lane boys.

Replacement of some of the glass panes heralded the start of repairing some of the war damage. This was organised by the Sheffield City architect, W.G. Davies.

Chapter Nine

A Long & Active Retirement

It seems likely that Willie met George Thomas, the future Speaker of the House of Commons, Viscount Tonypandy, at NUT executive meetings in London during the War. Peggy remembered that her father had said that Thomas would go far.

The January 1944 issue of *The Hallamshire Teacher – Wartime Series*, was the last of which Willie served on the editorial board. His final full year's salary as headmaster of Sharrow Lane School was £474. Then, at Christmas 1945 he retired at the age of sixty-one. Howard attributed his father's premature retirement to the demands and responsibilities brought about by the war. Willie received a cheque for an undisclosed sum from the Sheffield Teachers' Association and tributes by Ralph Morley and W.W. Hill were published in *The Hallamshire Teacher*.

Willie could certainly feel satisfied with what had been achieved at Sharrow Lane. Some sense of this could be gained from the fact that ten of Willie's assistant masters later gained headships in Sheffield.

With his teaching career over, Willie looked around for other outlets for his talents and considerable energy.

Attendance of a Sheffield City Council meeting dissuaded him from pursuing anything in local government, but around 1946 he became a founder member of the Sheffield Council of Churches.

Willie's nephew, Stanley Craddock, returned from front line war service abroad to his old employer, the mining tool manufacturer Hardy Pick. When a friend told him that he intended to train as a school teacher, Stanley joined him, commenced his career in Sheffield and joined the National Association of Schoolmasters. Throughout his long life, Stanley insisted that he was a schoolmaster whereas Willie considered himself to have been an educational facilitator. After many years of NUT service behind him, when they next met, Willie said 'Come here Stanley, you blighter'. That was, according to Stanley, the strongest language he had heard his uncle utter.

In June 1948, Willie, Edith and Peggy visited the Swart family in Groningen in the Netherlands. The effects of the wartime occupation were still evident so that the Robinson's presents of Sheffield cutlery and other items were very much appreciated by their old friends.

Willie and Edith's niece, Joan Craddock, married Philip Wade in September 1948. Ernest Craddock, daunted at the prospect of making a speech as the father of the bride, persuaded Willie to speak at the reception.

The following month, the eightieth anniversary of Hunsley Street chapel was celebrated by a tea. Willie, as secretary of the Trustees, presided and Mrs. Beighton, one of the oldest members was asked to cut the cake. Howard claimed that his parents had virtually run the chapel Sunday School for many years.

Tragedy struck Redcote ten days before Christmas in 1948 when Edith, who had suffered a stroke, died aged just sixty-five. Willie and Peggy received practical and moral support from the Swift family who had moved into 16 Crabtree Lane two years before. Willie's sister, Annie, visited Redcote once a week to provide what assistance she could.

As if to add to their distress, Hunsley Street chapel, where Willie's father had found Christian fellowship so many years before, closed during the following year. Willie and Peggy joined Trinity Methodist Church at Fir Vale and Willie was ultimately appointed the Society Steward.

During the early 1950s, Koos and Dien Swart and their sons, Felix and Peter, and old Mrs. Swart paid a visit to Redcote. (Old Mr. Swart had died in 1919 during the flu epidemic.)

In February 1956, Willie and Peggy held an eightieth birthday party for Annie at Redcote and took her to visit Howard and Margaret and their children, David and Christine, at their home in Folkestone. The following year, suffering from senile melancholia, Annie left her flat in the Crookes district of Sheffield for Redcote. Peggy was not at all content with the arrangement, but when Annie's condition deteriorated she entered Firvale Royal Infirmary. There Annie fell and broke her femur and died in January 1962 aged eighty-five.

Willie and Peggy spent Christmas Days with their neighbours, Barry and Marjory Swift and their children, Kathryn and Richard. On Boxing Days the Swifts went to Redcote and, occasionally in the evening, the Robinsons joined Ernest and May Craddock and their extended family at their bungalow, 14 Hemper Lane, in Bradway.

Willie developed an interest in Sheffield local history and made a collection of photographs of Old Crabtree. He was a regular visitor to the Central Library and Willie and Peggy invited numerous locals to Redcote to discuss his findings over tea.

Willie's involvement with the National Association of Youth Clubs (NAYC) was such that he was presented to Her Majesty the Queen Mother at St. James' Palace on the occasion of the Golden Jubilee in 1961. Although many youngsters found his quiet voice that tended to whistle through his teeth a little disconcerting, Willie's impish sense of humour usually won them over. He was often to be found sitting, puffing on his pipe and taking in all the arguments before making a considered statement. In November 1964, as Sheffield chairman of the NAYC, Willie received a long service award from the Hon. Angus Ogilvy.

In June of that year, Willie and Peggy again visited the Swart family and on 11th July an eightieth birthday party was held for Willie at Redcote. With a full house of Robinsons, Craddocks, friends and neighbours, the cake-board upon which eighty candles burned caused a little alarm. Some of the Trinity Church youngsters gave Willie and Peggy much practical help by revamping their garden as a surprise present.

With little ability or interest in practical things, in his old age Willie spent much of his time reading and listening to the radio. He told Barry Swift that he intended to continue to learn as long as he lived. As a result of their long discussions, Barry got to know much about Willie and his wealth of accumulated knowledge and wisdom.

Willie's brother-in-law, Ernest Craddock, died in January 1969.

Ernest's younger son, Peter and his family then lived in a large Edwardian house in Malvern where Willie and Peggy stayed the night on their way to their summer holiday in Tenby. A fortnight later they called in again on their return journey a few days prior to Willie's eighty-fifth birthday party at Redcote.

Willie and Peggy called in on the Craddocks in Malvern again in the summer of 1970. Then, in September father and daughter, along with 850 others, attended the NUT centenary dinner at the Guildhall in London. Peggy was most impressed by the speech given by the Secretary of State for Education, Margaret Thatcher.

Howard and Margaret's daughter, Christine, trained as a nurse at Great Ormond Street Hospital for Sick Children in London. In 1970 she met John Hassell, a fourth generation Australian, and emigrated to Australia in January of the following year. After Christine and John's marriage in Perth, Western Australia, Howard and Margaret also decided to emigrate to Australia.

David saw his parents leave the country on 10th June 1971. Howard was assured of a teaching post and Margaret, a part-time physiotherapist at the Royal Perth Hospital. Two days later Willie and Peggy stayed with the Craddocks in Malvern again when David briefly visited. The following November David took up a job with Orchard Motors in Singapore.

During the 1970s Willie was often accompanied to Sheffield Training College dinners by Stanley Craddock. It amused Stanley that visitors to Redcote were offered rolled-up newspapers with which to fend off their pet dog.

In 1971 Stanley's brother, Peter, and his family moved to Swansea. That could have been another stopping off point for Willie and Peggy when they visited Tenby in the summer of 1973. However, Peggy never drove on motorways and was daunted by the busy roads of South Wales.

Willie's ninetieth birthday in July 1974 was marked by another party at Redcote and a phone call from Howard, Margaret and family in Perth. By then Willie was a great-grandfather due to Christine and John Hassell's children Catherine (born in August 1972) and Mark (March 1974). About forty family and friends were present at Redcote including Koos, Dien and Steven Swart from Amsterdam.

In 1975 Willie and Peggy holidayed in Lowestoft and Beccles in Suffolk and Willie fell and dislocated his shoulder. Stanley Craddock visited Redcote to prune the buddleias and to help his uncle sort out his papers in his study over the garage. Some of the latter were given to the Training College archive but much was left to gather dust.

In December 1975 Willie and Peggy attended the STA centenary dinner at the Training College. It was attended by Fred Mulley, the Secretary of State for Education, and Sir Edward Britton, the former general secretary of the NUT. However, since Willie had been the president half a century earlier – indeed before the current president had been born – Willie was acknowledged as the Guest of Honour. This event was recorded in the *Morning Telegraph* in a story entitled 'Old Bill [Willie] and the Minister'.

That was a fitting climax to Willie's life for, less than two years later, on Sunday, 14th August 1977, he died at Redcote aged ninety-three. Four days later a Service of Thanksgiving was held at Trinity Methodist Church, a shorter service at Hutcliffe Wood Crematorium and yet another gathering at Redcote.

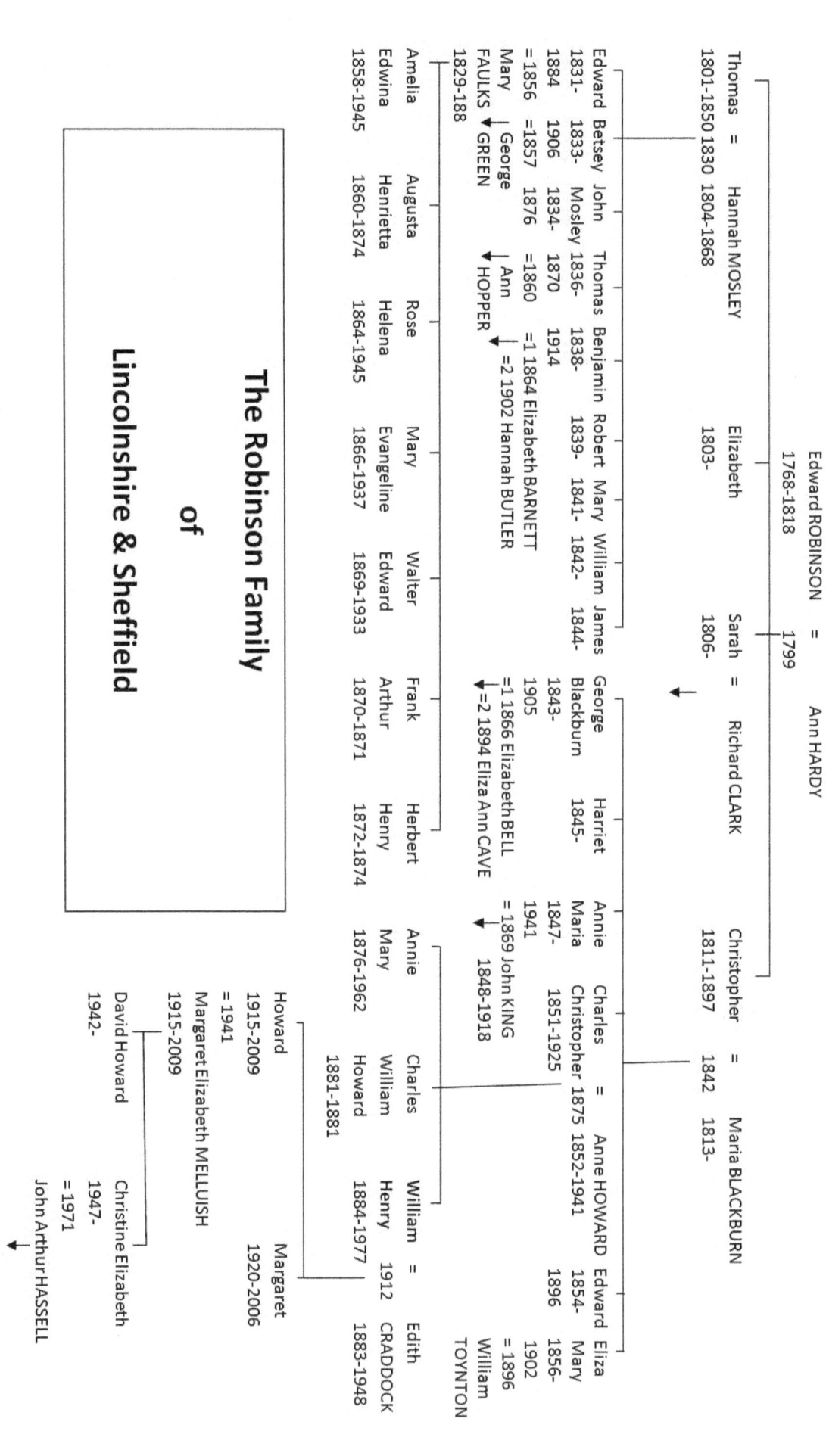

Willie Robinson as a young assistant schoolmaster

Willie & Edith's wedding, 29th May 1912

Rev. W.H. Brookes, Ernest Craddock, Charles Robinson, Nellie Craddock, Anne Robinson, Annie Robinson, Joseph Craddock, Edith Robinson, Catherine Craddock, Willie Robinson, Rev. V.W. Pearson & Bert Unwin

Howard, Edith, Annie & Willie Robinson, 1916

N.U.T. EXECUTIVE ELECTION, YORKSHIRE.

EASTER - - - 1928.

In order to ensure Proportional Representation, give first preference to

W. H. ROBINSON.

The Official Candidate of the N.F.C.T. and Y.F.C.T.
The only Candidate who is a Class Teacher.

Joan Craddock, Edith, Peggy, Willie, Stanley Craddock & Howard at Bridlington, 1929

Sheffield Independent

26th September 1931

National Federation of Class Teachers' Conference at Sheffield. Group includes Mr. W. N. Robinson, Alderman E. G. Rowlinson, the Lord Mayor, Mr. L. A. Grudgings, Mr. J. W. Connell (president), Mr. R. E. Sopwith and Mr. H. S. Newton.

John Smith, top boy in the examination, being congratulated by his headmaster at Sharrow lane School.

Sharrow Lane School, Sheffield, July 1934

NUT Conference at Margate, April 1938

Back row – Howard, Margaret Melluish, Peggy & Willie   Front row – Edith, Annie & Anne

Redcote, 14 Crabtree Lane, Sheffield, 1938

Howard & Margaret's wedding reception at Redcote, 1st November 1941

Willie & Edith with Christine, 1947

Willie & Peggy at Ernest & May Craddock's Ruby Wedding Anniversary, June 1960

Top row – Howard, Christine & DavidBottom Row – Peggy, Willie & Margaret

Willie's 80th birthday party, Redcote, 11th July 1964

Willie being presented with a National Association of Youth Clubs long service award

by the Hon. Angus Ogilvy, November 1964

Willie with John, Philip & Kay Craddock, Malvern, 8th June 1969

Willie & David Robinson, Kay Craddock & Peggy Robinson

Malvern, 12th June 1971

Willie & Peggy prior to the NUT Centenary dinner at the Guildhall, London, September 1970

Willie & Peggy prior to the Sheffield Teachers' Association Centenary dinner, 5th December 1975

Bibliography

Adsetts Library Special Collection, Sheffield Hallam University,
W.H. Robinson's papers on education in Sheffield
    The Ilond 1919-1929
    Newspaper cuttings on scholarship exam, 1922, 1923 & 1929
    Sheffield Education Week, 16-22 Nov 1924
    National Union of Teachers, West Yorks County Association,
        Memoranda on A National System of Education,
            The Presidential Address of W.H. Robinson [hand-written on the cover] 1925
    Sharrow Lane Council School, The Jubilee of the School, Feb 1937
    First Rough Draft of Notes (Unrevised) For an Account of Sharrow Lane Boys' School,
                              Feb 1941 to Jan 1943, by W.H. Robinson

The National Archives
ED 21/45141	Huntsman's Gardens Council School	1923-1929
ED 21/45165	Pipworth Road Council School	1929-1931
ED 21/45198	Sharrow Lane Council School	1931-1935
ED 21/65893	Sharrow Lane Council School	1936-1944

Christine Elizabeth Hassell
Documents & photographs including –
    Newspaper articles concerning W.H. Robinson
    The Ilond 1919-1929
    Margaret Robinson's memoirs 1996 & 2001

Sheffield Archives
NR 2321/1	Hunsley Street Baptism Register	1915 & 1920
2004/17	Sheffield Teachers' Association minute books	1937-1946
School Log Books		
CA 35/14	Newhall Junior	1904-1912
CA 35/31	Newhall Senior Mixed	1909-1911
CA 35/103	Grimesthorpe Board Boys' Department	1903-1906 & 1911-1914
CA 35/760 & 761	Huntsman's Gardens	1919-1929
2010/102	Pipworth Road Council Senior Mixed	1929-1931

Sheffield Local Studies Library
        Sheffield directories & electoral rolls
371.1S The Hallamshire Teacher,
        The Organ of the Sheffield and District Teachers' Association NUT,
            New Series No.1 Jan 1927 – No.53 Mar 1940
            Wartime Series No.1 May 1941 – No.27 Nov 1945
379.4274SST City of Sheffield Education Week Handbooks & Programmes, 1924, 1927 & 1935
PAMP 929/2S Official opening of four Council Schools, (including Pipworth Road) 3 Oct 1929
        Sheffield Association of Youth Clubs 38th annual report, 1977-8

Society of Genealogists
Lincolnshire Parish Registers   Lusby Mf 1269   Revesby Mf 1513   Leake Mf 2672 & 2673
Teachers' Registration Council Register, W.H. Robinson, 1 Sep 1920, Register No. 56670

Books

High Storrs School – A Journey, Arc Publishing & Print, 2011

The W.E.A. Education Year Book 1918, The Workers' Educational Association, London,
'The Sheffield Teachers' Education Campaign of 1917' by W.H. Robinson p 447-448

Armytage, W.H.G., Four Hundred Years of English Education, Cambridge at the University Press, 1970

Bayliss et al, Building Schools for Sheffield 1870-1914, The Victorian Society, 2012

Bourne & MacArthur, The Struggle for Education 1870-1970, Schoolmaster Publishing Co., n.d.

Cook, H. Caldwell, The Play Way, An Essay in Educational Method, William Heinemann, London, 1917

Findlay, J.J., The Foundations of Education, University of London Press, 1930

License, Paul, Sheffield Blitz, Sheffield Newspapers Ltd., 2000

Morton, Ann, Education and the State from 1833, PRO Publications, 1997

Robinson, W.H., The Teachers' ABC, Sheffield Independent Press, 1911

Young, Ernest, editor, The New Era in Education, George Philip & Son, [no date but probably 1922]
XXVII The Sheffield Federated Education Association by O.M. Andrews p 241-247
adapted from material supplied by the Secretary of the Association [W.H. Robinson]

Thesis

Elcock, Audrey Anne, Government Evacuation Schemes and their Effect on School Children
in Sheffield during the Second World War, Ph.D., University of Sheffield, 1999

Journals

Robinson, W.H., Our Ilond Community, The Journal of Experimental Pedagogy, vol 5 no 6, 6 Dec 1920

Mr. William H. Robinson, The Joint Magazine of the Fir Vale Churches St. Cuthbert's and Trinity,
March 1971

Newspapers

The British Newspaper Archive and other Internet databases enable searches by keyword, title, place of publication and date range. The extensive use of these databases employed during research for this book is such that little is to be gained by listing all of these references.

www.ingramcontent.com/pod-product-compliance
Lightning Source LLC
Chambersburg PA
CBHW081600040426
42446CB00014B/3223